Her Wandering Words

Hanna Grover

Presentation by *BookLeaf Publishing*

Web: www.bookleafpub.com

E-mail: info@bookleafpub.com

ISBN: 978-93-95784-14-6

First edition 2022

DEDICATION

For myself, to a new era of self reflection and change.

PREFACE

"she lives the poetry she cannot write"

- Oscar Wilde

the layers between us

compassion.

our friendship is like two stars colliding
we both look to make sure the other is okay
and without hesitation
we apologize
no matter who had the faulty ways

comfort.

our friendship is like a square with no walls,
we try and search for the corners,
but are distracted in the endless maze
and end up laughing
in each other's space

carefree.

our friendship is like the indigo blue waters
we like to go with the flow
but take the risk to stop and
enjoy the gentle waves,
nice and slow

complete.

our friendship is like a hidden outfit,
discovered before date night
each stitch and seam
hugs you just right

our bond, dear friend
is still an unexplainable mystery
and sometimes
that is the best part.

a complex definition

you are the essence of literature
and poetry in its
purest form
i cannot describe you
with one word,
but rather
a million metaphors.

back to life

there were days when i could not grow
until someone
came to water my feet
until i was strong enough
to rise on my own

there were days where i was cold
until someone
gave me warmth
like how the sun
warms her creations

there were days where i felt alone
like one lone flower in a muddy field
until someone
tore me from the muddy ground
and planted me
in the right
place

who was this someone
having such a dear heart
who would give so selflessly

it was my sister
who nourished me
back to life.

the perfect dress

5

she delicately stitched
her wounds
and faults
into a piece of fine lace
and wore her imperfections
with pride and brace.

.

women

women is like the soil

women is the soil that nurtures the plant
women is the soil that creates
growth
women is the soil that is the
base of all
success

women is like water

women is the water that is
home to many beings
women is the water that keeps the world
alive
women is the water that is always
flowing

women is like fire

women is the fire who is always blazing
women is the fire,
 a burning desire

women is the air

women is the air who is always there
women is the air that you
need to stay
vital
women is the air,
the root of life

women is the earth.

the elements we need to
survive
thrive
and energize our planet

so it is time to unite
unite man and woman, woman and man
unite as one planet
unite the four elements of our
earth

because women,
are equal.

two sides

some people struggle in chaos
and that is how they grow
but
some people thrive in chaos
because chaos is all they know.

to my parents

they are sunshine

their energy, warm and welcoming
especially on gloomy days
their smile, bright and optimistic
just like the golden rays

they are water

the endless flow of support
has meant the world, you see
like an ocean with its waves
being home to animals in the sea

they are soil

the unwavered determination and commitment
to ground and nourish my roots
your flexibility and understanding
are just one of your many admirable attributes

they are my parents

everything you could ever hope for in a person
and all the elements responsible for my growth
words are just simply not enough
my heart is filled with gratitude
and so much endless love.

where the truth lives

deep down
within the many layers of our identity
that we put on display
lies a mystery dwelling
in black and white,
the realization
that nobody will know you
like you do
yourself.

my sanctuary

she stared at her bed
and bent over to
feel
the rigid fibers of the blanket
remembering that it once was
soft and youthful
like her childhood

she stared at the four walls
that enclosed her
pictures and colors
the rush of nostalgia
like water on a camera lens
softening all the memories
that kept replaying
in her mind

she stared at the ceiling
each engravement on the wood
each groove and crack
telling a tale
like a scattered story

she stared at the door
the one in which she slammed
many times
in anger
and sorrow
almost as if she could feel
the raging fire of emotions
burning her
to shrivels

the girl stood
in the middle of
her room
and felt safe
her walls were her shields
her ceiling was her helmet
her bed was her storm cellar

her room was her sanctuary
that she didn't know she had.

excusing ourselves

we dream of success
and prosperity
like the shine of gold
but only put in the effort
to reach a silver
and we wonder
why we have tarnished
into a bronze.

her

i look into the mirror, and what do i see?

a gentle baby girl staring back at me
soft supple skin,
and hazel brown eyes
she's wearing a blue gingham dress,
one that simply cannot be despised

i look into the mirror, and what do i see?

a cheerful little girl staring back at me
a sweet toothless smile
and a fun hair style
she's throwing paper planes
and constantly rolling around getting grass stains

i look into the mirror and what do i see?

a sweet preteen staring back at me
scrolling on screens
and trying to fit in,
she's wanting to understand
who she is from within

she looks away from the mirror,
uncertainty in her eyes
her future is approaching, her childhood flying
by

i look into the mirror and what do i see?

the image is blurry, who will i be
carefree
fun
grounded
i finally want to be free

as the years go by
i hope the future will comply
because i think it is time
to unfold the inner child
 in me.

salt and sugar

don't confuse
salt for sugar
if it was meant to work out
it would've
but instead you're left with
a bittersweet recipe.

royalty

she has blue eyes
you have brown
her's represent the sea,
yours are the ground

she has long blonde hair
you have black
told they look like the glistening sun
but yours are taken aback

she has soft eurocentric features
you have bold
her's are yearned over
but yours look old

but dear friend,

your eyes are a gem that will bring unforeseen fame
your hair is as black as the ace of spades,
undoubtedly the highest value in the game
your features bring stares,
people admiring your beauty with a silent glare

your being
reigns like a queen
and you hold the purest riches
the universe has ever seen.

optical illusion

who are you
without the glamorized version
others see

who are you
when you stop searching
for instant validation in everything

who are you
when you start doing things
for yourself

who are you
when nobody is watching?

reality of fear

you are not afraid of the future
you are afraid of uncertainty
not knowing what the future holds for you
unsure whether or not you'll be good enough
sometimes wondering how you'll make it out in
the world of monsters
whom only a few are kind among them

you are not afraid of commitment
you are afraid of being hurt once again
pouring your heart into something just for it to
turn out like the others
gone
the feeling of having someone by your side
quickly vanish without warning.

you are not afraid of the past
you are afraid of the repetitiveness
the same mistakes happening, over and over
the same moments, rewinding themselves like a
broken record
the same feelings, rushing back, when you
thought they would never come again

you are not afraid of missing out
you are afraid of being forgotten
the fear of knowing that your presence never
mattered
so perhaps your absence won't be noticed.

needs

you can live without self love
like a plant lives without water
but in the end
they both turn dead and brittle
regardless if they can "survive"
without it.

evolving emotions

pride is amber
it sounds like laughter in the summer, the late
night fun
it tastes like the first bite into a warm pie, freshly
baked
it smells like the crisp fall air, the wind blowing
in your hair
pride feels like the moment when you score
perfect marks, your heart squeezing with joy

this pride turns into regret, the amber changing
to grey

regret is grey
it sounds like a person trapped inside an empty
room, calling for help
it tastes like bitter candy, left over from
halloween
it smells like an empty house filled with dust,
being abandoned for decades
regret feels like the gut-wrenching feeling of a
bullet stuck in your intestine

envy is emerald green
it sounds like a train approaching the station, the
closer it gets, the more deafening it becomes
it tastes like yew berries, sweet, but deadly
it smells like burning embers
envy feels like falling into a deep hole, with no
way out

this envy turns into inspiration, changing from
emerald green to light blue

inspiration is light blue
it sounds like birds chirping on an early sunday
morning
it tastes like sweet strawberries, freshly grown
from your own garden
it smells like your birthday cake, coming straight
out of the oven
inspiration feels like fuel to a fire

uncertainty is white
it sounds like blurred shouts, unable to hear the
words
it tastes like bland food, flavorless
it smells like humid air on a rainy day
uncertainty feels like balancing on a wire,
unsure of what will happen

this uncertainty turns to acceptance, the white
changing to blue

acceptance is blue
it sounds like cheers from the side-lines when
you score in a basketball game
it tastes like cheesecake, not too sweet, but not
too bland
it smells like fresh bloomed flowers from the
start of spring
acceptance feels like the warm sand beneath
your toes on a warm summer day

justice for mother nature

ocean
the tranquil waves, whispering me to the limitless
sand
the glistening sun, bouncing off the indigo waters
little do we know, a deep truth lies beneath them
the ocean full of being, washes up death on its shore
the sea animals we admire from afar, now choking on
the plastic that plunders

sky
the clouds, different shapes, different pictures
the splash of blue that brings us joy
the whistling breeze, running through our hair
our skies now blackened, the clouds now grey
the air we breathe,
dirty

trees
the years of stories they tell
the oxygen they provide
the pillars of the forest, now teared down
by nobody,
but us

soil
the blanket that lies beneath our feet
and the home of many
a symbol of growth, perseverance, and patience
now treated with nothing
but disrespect

sun
the light that brightens our darkest days
and one that hugs the greenery with love and strength
an energy never before seen now evolved into a
raging glare
our temperatures incomprehensible, leaving burning
embers behind

earth
Mother Nature is weeping, each element now
destroyed
as we've torn down the beauty she created
now we must come together to reflect on our
mistakes
and hand out justice
all before
it's too late.